Strange ... But True?

VAMPIRES

XINA M. UHL

⊕ WORLD BOOK

This World Book edition of *Vampires* is published by agreement between Black Rabbit Books and World Book, Inc.
© 2018 Black Rabbit Books,
2140 Howard Dr. West,
North Mankato, MN 56003 U.S.A.
World Book, Inc.,
180 North LaSalle St., Suite 900,
Chicago, IL 60601 U.S.A.

Marysa Storm, editor; Grant Gould, interior designer; Michael Sellner, cover designer; Omay Ayres, photo researcher

Library of Congress Control Number: 2016049987

ISBN: 978-0-7166-9357-4

Printed in the United States at CG Book Printers,
North Mankato, Minnesota, 56003. 3/17

BOLT

Image Credits
Alamy: captblack76, 6 (face); Granamour Weems Collection, 21 (top); Historical image collection by Bildagentur-online, Mary Evans Picture Library, 13; Getty Images: Frederick M. Brown, 21 (bottom); Johner Images, 10 (bat); Najin, Cover; http://mno.hu/: Unkown, 14; iStock: Lowe- Stock, 6, 9; Shutterstock: Algol, 10–11; Annie Dove, 28–29; antoniomas, 26; artshock, 16–17; chippix, 25; Cristian Balate, 32; irin-k, 6 (flame), 23 (flame); Jerax, 22 (vampire); Kiselev An- drey Valerevich, 1, Back Cover; Olemac, 23 (sword); tsuneomp, 31; Vera Petruk, 23 (stake); Zaracrias Pereira da Mata, 3
Every effort has been made to contact copyright holders for material reproduced in this book. Any omissions will be rectified in subsequent printings if notice is given to the publisher.

Contents

CHAPTER 1

The

In 1892, a man named Edwin Brown became deathly ill. The townspeople wondered if his sister was to blame. Mercy Lena Brown had died a few months earlier. The townspeople worried she was a vampire. They had no other way to explain Edwin's condition. They dug up Mercy's grave. Her body was still fresh!

Vampire Tales

Some of the townspeople said Mercy's fingernails had grown. Others said she wasn't in the same position she had been buried in. The townspeople were sure she was a vampire. They cut out her heart and burned it.

The Browns' story is one of many vampire tales. In fact, people have told stories about these creatures for hundreds of years.

A group of vampires is called a coven or clan.

Monsters Among Us

Stories say vampires have pale skin. They hate garlic, and sunlight hurts them. They run from religious crosses. Holy water burns them. Many stories say vampires have cold skin. They say the creatures can't be seen in mirrors. Some stories say vampires **communicate** with animals. Others say they can turn into bats.

Vampire **traits** vary from story to story. But one trait always stays the same. Vampires drink blood.

VAMPIRE FEATURES

CHANGES INTO BAT

FANGS

BLOOD AT MOUTH

PALE SKIN

SLEEPS IN COFFIN OR GRAVE

throughout History

Vampire stories date back hundreds of years. They come from India, China, and Europe. To **ancient** people, blood gave a person life. Some believed drinking blood could give a person power. This idea may have started vampire **legends**. But could actual vampires be behind the stories?

13

Dracul means "dragon" or "devil" in the Romanian language.

Real Vampires?

Some stories may come from real people, such as Vlad Tepes. This prince lived in Transylvania in the 1400s. He was nicknamed Vlad Dracula. He was known for **impaling** enemies on stakes.

Elizabeth Bathory lived in the late 1500s in Hungary. She wanted to stay young. To do so, she killed many girls. Then she drank their blood. Bathory became known as the "Blood Countess."

VAMPIRES AROUND THE WORLD

Vampire stories are told around the world. Names and traits vary from place to place.

ALBANIA
shtriga

UNITED STATES
vampire

TOGO & GHANA
adze

RUSSIA
upyr

GREECE
lamiai

CHINA
jiangshi

A Serbian Story

In the early 1700s, a man returned home to a town in Serbia. His name was Arnold. He said he had been bitten by a vampire in Greece. His neighbors began to worry. Shortly after he returned, Arnold died. Stories tell that others began to die soon after he did. His neighbors decided to dig up Arnold's **corpse**. They found blood coming out of its mouth.

CHAPTER 3

A Popular

In 1897, Bram Stoker **published** *Dracula*. A movie with the same name came out in 1931. The book and movie featured Count Dracula. He was a pale man who wore a black cloak. Fangs grew in his mouth. He could turn into a bat. Vampire popularity has grown since then.

Today, most vampire stories come from TV shows and movies. Vampires are in a lot of books too.

Count Von Count stars on *Sesame Street.* He looks like Count Dracula. But he doesn't like to bite necks. He prefers to count numbers instead.

How Do You Kill a

Stories say killing a vampire isn't easy.
A person needs the right tools for the job.

SUNLIGHT

FIRE

STAKE
TO DRIVE
THROUGH HEART

SWORD
TO CHOP OFF HEAD

23

CHAPTER 4

Explaining

Many people don't believe vampires are real. They think science can explain the stories. As dead bodies **decay**, the skin becomes dry. Teeth and fingernails seem longer. Blood can leak from their mouths and eyes.

Illnesses could also explain vampires. Porphyria makes people pale. Light bothers their eyes. Catalepsy makes people seem dead. Later, they may awaken.

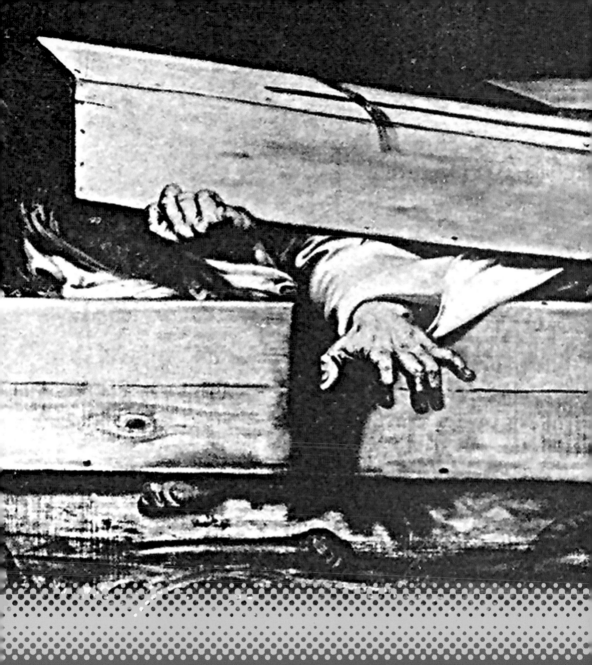

A person with porphyria avoids garlic.
Eating it causes great pain.

Real or Fake?

Many people believe vampires are made-up. They say people didn't always understand how bodies decayed. They think vampires were used to explain death and disease.

Others aren't so sure. Some people think the old tales are true. They believe vampires don't exist in just movies and books.

What do you think?

Believe It or Not?

Answer the questions below.
Then add up your points to
see if you believe.

1 **It is night. You see a pale man in the cemetery. What do you think?**

A. I better find some garlic! (3 points)

B. That's strange. (2 points)

C. It's probably someone working.
(1 point)

2 You see a bat at your window. What's your first thought?

A. Vampire! (3 points)

B. As long as it stays out, I'm OK. (2 points)

C. It's just a bat. (1 point)

3 Your friend refuses to eat garlic bread. What do you think?

A. She's a vampire! (3 points)

B. That's weird. Garlic bread is the best! (2 points)

C. So what? (1 point)

. . . .

3 points
There's no way you think vampires are real.

4–8 points
Maybe they're real. But then again, maybe they're not.

9 points
You're a total believer!

ancient (AYN-shunt)—from a time long ago

communicate (kuh-MYU-nuh-kayt)—to share information, thoughts, or feelings so that they are understood

corpse (KORPS)—a dead body

decay (dee-KAY)—to rot away

impale (im-PEYL)—to cause a pointed object to go into or through something or someone

legend (LEJ-uhnd)—a story from the past that cannot be proved true

publish (PUHB-lish)—to prepare and produce a book or magazine for sale

trait (TREYT)—a characteristic or quality

BOOKS

Felix, Rebecca. *Vampires.* Creatures of Legend. Minneapolis: ABDO Publishing Company, 2014.

Larson, Kirsten W. *Vampires in Nature.* Freaky Nature. Mankato, MN: Amicus High Interest, 2016.

Loh-Hagan, Virginia. *Vampires: Magic, Myth, and Mystery.* Magic, Myth, and Mystery. Ann Arbor, MI: Cherry Lake Publishing, 2017.

WEBSITES

The Legend of Vampires
www.kidzworld.com/article/24861-the-legend-of-vampires

Monster 101: All About Vampires
www.cbc.ca/kidscbc2/the-feed/monsters-101-all-about-vampires

Vampire Bat
kids.nationalgeographic.com/animals/vampire-bat/#vampire-bat-flying-wings.jpg

INDEX